Song indexed West.

Production: Sadie Cook

Music processed by Global Music Solutions, Surrey SM6 9BT

Cover design by Headline Publicity Limited

Published 1997

AC-CENT-TCHU-ATE THE POSITIVE

Words by JOHNNY MERCER
Music by HAROLD ARLEN

ANYTHING YOU CAN DO

Words and Music by IRVING BERLIN

BE A CLOWN

Words and Music by COLE PORTER

BLUES IN THE NIGHT

Words by JOHNNY MERCER
Music by HAROLD ARLEN

BEYOND THE SEA (LA MER)

Original Words and Music by CHARLES TRENET
English Words by JACK LAWRENCE

THE BOY NEXT DOOR

Words and Music by HUGH MARTIN and RALPH BLANE

B♭maj7　Gm7　C11　C7　Cm7

love him more than I can say.＿＿＿＿ Does-n't try to
love her more than I can say.＿＿＿＿ Does-n't try to

F9　B♭　Gm7　Em7♭5　A7

please me,　does-n't ev - en tease me,　and he ne - ver sees me
please me,　does-n't ev - en tease me,　and she ne - ver sees me

Dm　D♭dim7　Cm7　F9　B♭maj7　G7　Cm7

glance his way.＿ And though I'm heart - sore the boy next
glance her way.＿ And though I'm heart - sore the girl next

CHATTANOOGA CHOO CHOO

Words by MACK GORDON
Music by HARRY WARREN

Par - don me boy _____ is that the Cha - ta - noo - ga choo - choo, _____ track twen - ty - nine, _____ boy you can gim - me a shine? _____

CHOO CHOO CH'BOOGIE

Words and Music by DENVER DARLING, MILTON GABLER
and VAUGHN HORTON

choo— ch' boo – gie, take me right back to the track, jack!

Take me right back to the track, jack!

DO NOTHIN' TILL YOU HEAR FROM ME

Words by BOB RUSSELL
Music by DUKE ELLINGTON

DON'T SIT UNDER THE APPLE TREE

Words and Music by LEW BROWN, CHARLES TOBIAS
and SAM STEPT

I come march-ing home._____ I

(see additional lyric)

just got word from the guy who heard from the guy next door to
told the gang, from the whole she- bang, from that guy you were sweet and

me, the girl he met just loves to pet and it
true, they ran right out and came right back with a

fits you to a 'T.' So! Don't sit un-der the ap-ple tree with
pho- to- graph of you.

44

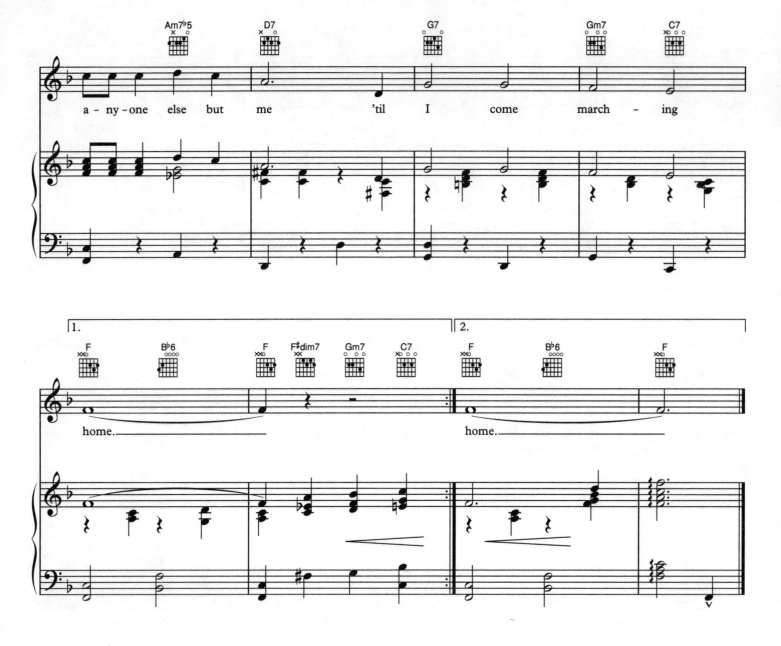

a - ny - one else but me 'til I come march - ing home.

home.

Though navy blue may appeal to you when you meet a bold Jack Tar
Don't be a sport when the fleet's in port 'cos you know what sailors are. So!

Be dumb and deaf when the R.A.F. say 'The moon is shining bright!'
They might take sips from your red lips as 'The target for tonight!' So!

That apple tree knows the history of our meetings after dark
I'd hate to find other names entwined with yours, upon the bark. So!

You sat with me 'neath the apple tree when I stole our first love kiss
I won't deny Ma's apple pie ain't the only thing I miss. So!

EVERYBODY LOVES SOMEBODY

Words by IRVING TAYLOR
Music by KEN LANE

Some-where there's a - no-ther heart to warm a heart that's cold;

Some-one's hand is wait-ing for a lone-ly hand to hold.

Ev - 'ry dream-er has a dream that

ELMER'S TUNE

Words and Music by ELMER ALBRECHT, SAMMY GALLOP
and DICK JURGENS

El - mer____ de - ci - ded that he____ would write a lit - tle mel - o - dy;____
Moz - art____ with - out a - ny doubt a - way from all this care and strife____

Yes sir,____ he fin - ished it soon and now they're sing - in' El - mer's tune.____ Why are the
knows that____ he ne - ver turned out____ a tune like this in all his life.____

GOD BLESS THE CHILD

Words and Music by ARTHUR HERZOG JR and BILLIE HOLIDAY

GUESS I'LL HANG MY TEARS OUT TO DRY

Words by SAMMY CAHN
Music by JULE STYNE

Strange - ly en - ough,__ I got a - long with - out him, her,

then one day he passed me right by,__ oh well, I guess I'll hang my tears out to dry.

cresc.

1. 2.

mf mf

HARLEM NOCTURNE

Words by DICK ROGERS
Music by EARLE HAGEN

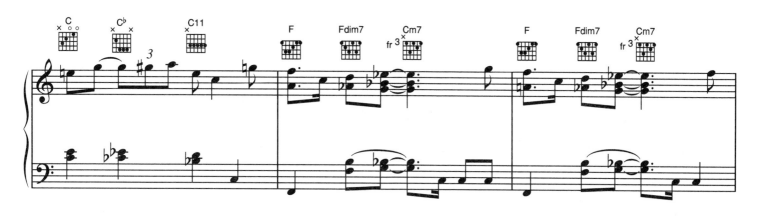

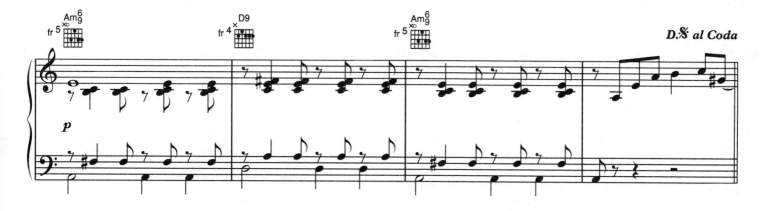

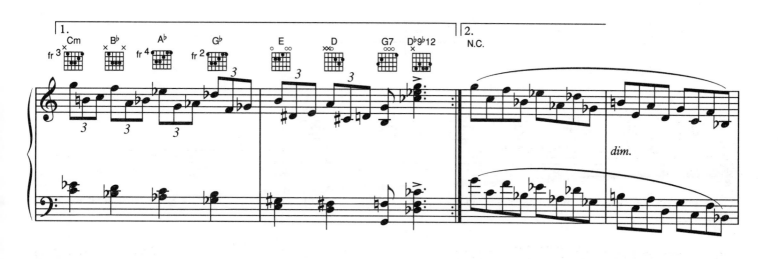

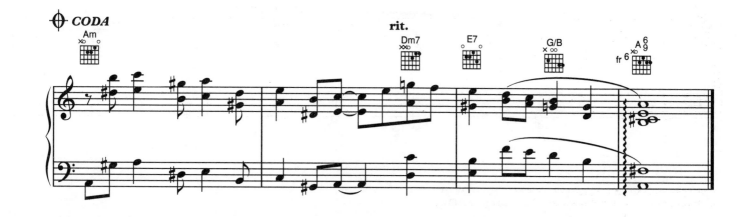

I GOT IT BAD AND THAT AIN'T GOOD

Words by PAUL FRANCIS WEBSTER
Music by DUKE ELLINGTON

I'M BEGINNING TO SEE THE LIGHT

Words and Music by HARRY JAMES, DUKE ELLINGTON,
JOHNNY HODGES and DON GEORGE

Medium bounce

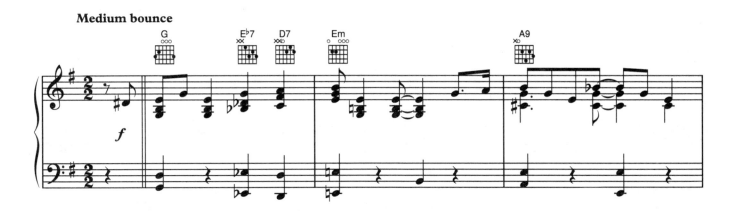

I ne-ver cared much for moon-lit skies, I ne-ver wink back at

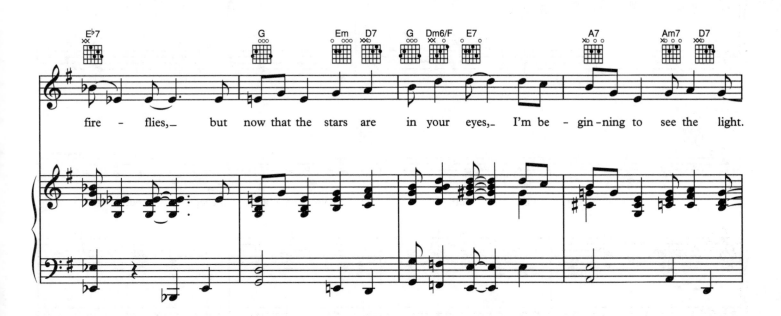

fire - flies,__ but now that the stars are in your eyes,__ I'm be - gin-ning to see the light.

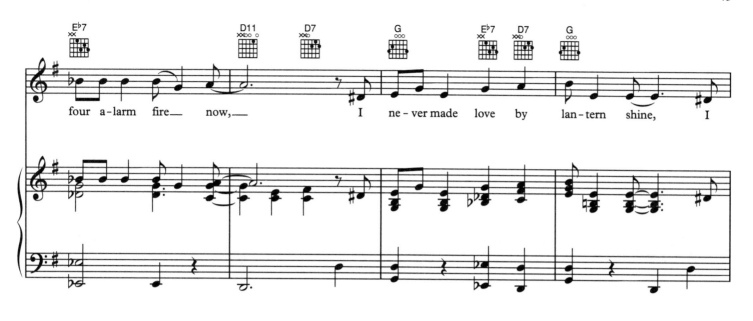

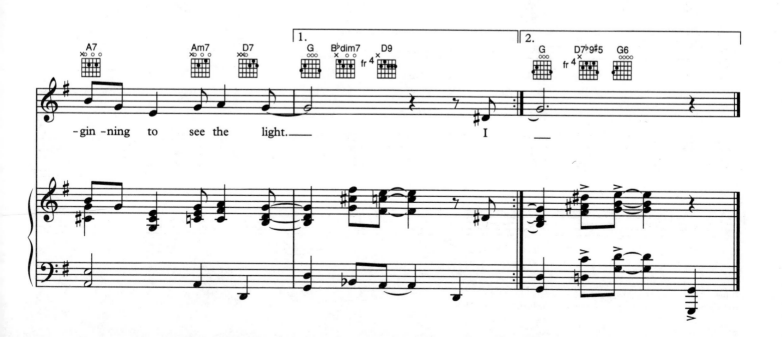

IT'S A GREAT DAY FOR THE IRISH

Words and Music by ROGER EDENS

for sure you'd think New York was Old Kil - lar - ney!

be - go - ra all the cops are out pa - ra - ding!

It's a great day for the sham - rock,

It's a great day for the sham - rock,

for the flags in full ar - ray.

for the flags in full ar - ray.

LAVENDER BLUE (DILLY DILLY)

Words by LARRY MOREY
Music by ELIOT DANIEL

JAVA JIVE

Words by MILTON DRAKE
Music by BEN OAKLAND

JUST A-SITTIN' AND A-ROCKIN'

Words by LEE GAINES
Music by BILLY STRAYHORN and DUKE ELLINGTON

MOONLIGHT IN VERMONT

Words by JOHN M BLACKBURN
Music by KARL SUESSDORF

Pen-nies in a stream, fal-ling leaves, a sy-ca-more, moon-light in Ver-mont. I-cy fin-ger waves, ski trails on a mount-ain -side, snow-light in Ver - mont. Te-le-graph ca - bles, they sing down the high-way and

NATURE BOY

Words and Music by EDEN AHBEZ

OLD DEVIL MOON

Words by E Y HARBURG
Music by BURTON LANE

ON GREEN DOLPHIN STREET

Words by NED WASHINGTON
Music by BRONISLAU KAPER

ON THE ATCHISON, TOPEKA AND THE SANTA FE

Words by JOHNNY MERCER
Music by HARRY WARREN

ONE FOR MY BABY
(AND ONE MORE FOR THE ROAD)

Words by JOHNNY MERCER
Music by HAROLD ARLEN

PENNSYLVANIA 6-5000

Words and Music by CARL SIGMAN and JERRY GRAY

ROUTE 66

Words and Music by BOBBY TROUP

go thro' Saint Lou - is and Jop - lin, Mis-sour-i and Ok - la - ho - ma Ci - ty is might-

- ty pret-ty; you'll see___ A - ma - ril - lo;___ Gal - lup, New

Mex - i - co;___ Flag-staff, A - ri - zo - na; don't for - get Wi - no - na,

King - man, Bar - stow, San Ber - nar - di - no. Won't you___ get hip

'ROUND MIDNIGHT

Words and Music by COOTIE WILLIAMS and THELONIOUS MONK

SKYLARK

Words by JOHNNY MERCER
Music by HOAGY CARMICHAEL

SOMEONE'S ROCKING MY DREAMBOAT

Words and Music by LEON RENE, OTIS RENE and EMERSON SCOTT

SPEAK LOW

Words by OGDEN NASH
Music by KURT WEILL

STEPPIN' OUT WITH MY BABY

Words and Music by IRVING BERLIN

Medium jump tempo

If I seem to scin-til-late,__ it's be-cause I've got a date,__

a date with a pack-age of__ the good things that come with love.__

You don't have to ask me,__ I won't waste your time.

A SUNDAY KIND OF LOVE

Words and Music by BARBARA BELLE, ANITA LEONARD,
STAN RHODES and LOUIS PRIMA

I want a Sun - day kind of love,— a love to last past Sa - tur day night, I'd like to know it's more than love at first sight,

A STRING OF PEARLS

Words by EDDIE DeLANGE
Music by JERRY GRAY

Ba - by,___ here's___ a five and dime. ba - by,___ now's
Ba - by,___ you___ made quite a start, found the___ way
I___

___ a - bout the time for a___ string___ of pearls a la
___ right to my heart with a___ string___ of pearls a la

TAKE THE "A" TRAIN

Words and Music by BILLY STRAYHORN

TICO-TICO (TICO-TICO NO FUBA)

Portuguese Words by ALOYSIO OLIVEIRA
English Words by ERVIN DRAKE
Music by ZEQUINHA ABREU

Oh, Ti-co - ti-co tick!_ Oh, Ti-co - ti-co tock!_ This Ti-co -
O Ti-co - ti-co tá,_ tá ou-tra vez a-qui,_ o Ti-co -

-ti-co he's the cuck-oo in my clock. And when he says: 'Cuck-oo!'_ he means it's
-ti-co tá co-men-do o meu fu-bá. Si o Ti-co-ti-co tem,_ tem que se a

time to woo;_ It's 'Ti-co-time' for all the lov-ers in the block. I've got a
li-men-tar,_ Que vá co-mer u-mas mi-nho-cas no po-mar. O Ti-co-

TOO DARN HOT

Words and Music by COLE PORTER

YOU STEPPED OUT OF A DREAM

Words by GUS KAHN
Music by NACIO HERB BROWN

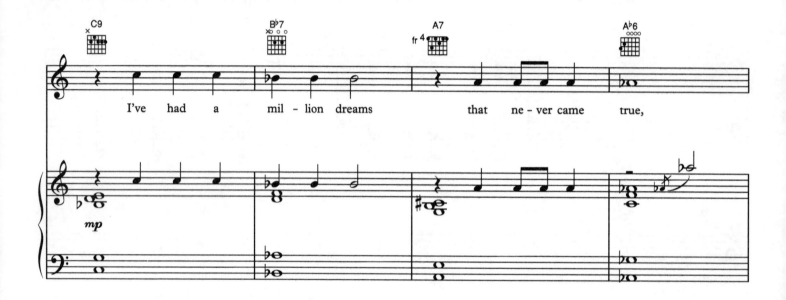

I've had a mil-lion dreams that ne-ver came true,

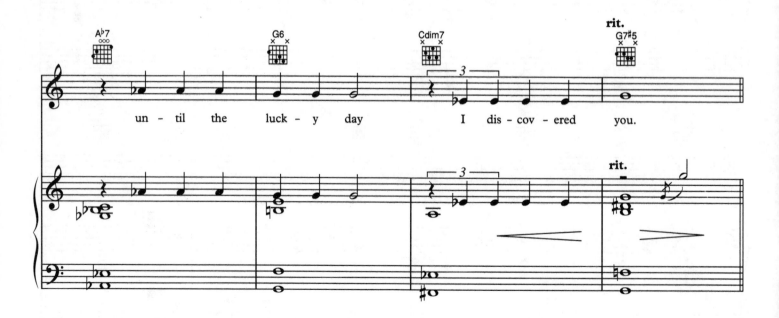

un-til the luck-y day I dis-cov-ered you.

Printed in Great Britain by Hobbs the Printers Ltd, Totton, Hampshire 11/97